DATE DUE

NOV 2 1 2023	
DISCARDED	
	PRINTED IN U.S.A.

THE HORSE LIBRARY

HORSE BREEDS OF THE WORLD

BRENT KELLEY

CHELSEA HOUSE PUBLISHERS

PHILADELPHIA

Frontis: **The Arab is one of the oldest and purest horse breeds in the world.**

CHELSEA HOUSE PUBLISHERS

EDITOR IN CHIEF Sally Cheney
ASSOCIATE EDITOR IN CHIEF Kim Shinners
PRODUCTION MANAGER Pamela Loos
ART DIRECTOR Sara Davis

STAFF FOR *HORSE BREEDS OF THE WORLD*

EDITOR Sally Cheney
ASSOCIATE ART DIRECTOR Takeshi Takahashi
SERIES DESIGNER Keith Trego

CHESTNUT PRODUCTIONS AND CHOPTANK SYNDICATE, INC.

EDITORIAL AND PICTURE RESEARCH Mary Hull and Norman Macht
LAYOUT AND PRODUCTION Lisa Hochstein

http://www.chelseahouse.com

First Printing

1 3 5 7 9 8 6 4 2

Library of Congress Cataloguing-in-Publication Data Applied For.

Horse Library SET: 0-7910-6650-9
Horse Breeds of the World: 0-7910-6652-5

TABLE OF CONTENTS

Heavy horses like the Shire are the ancestors of the horses that developed in the northern half of Europe and Asia during the Ice Age. Because they had to survive harsh winters on minimal feed sources, these animals grew thick coats and large, heavy bodies with a protective layer of fat. They came to be known as "cold-blooded" horses.

EVOLUTION OF
THE HORSE

The great Secretariat, a Thoroughbred racehorse, won the Triple Crown and was syndicated for millions of dollars. Secretariat was no accident. He was the culmination of millions of years of evolution and hundreds of years of selective breeding. He is just one example of what horses have become.

There are more than 400 breeds of horses around the world, ranging in size from the six-foot tall draft horses, some of which can weigh a ton and a half, to miniature horses smaller than dogs. All of them, however, came from a common ancestor, an animal called Hyracotherium, which was about the size of a fox.

Hyracotherium lived 60 to 70 million years ago. It was a vegetarian, like all members of the family, and lived in swampy forests where it was a browser. It had three toes on its hind feet and four on its forefeet.

By 25 to 35 million years ago, Mesohippus appeared. This was an animal about the size of a sheep, with only three toes on its front feet.

Easy prey for meat eaters, these prehistoric ancestors of the horse moved to the open grasslands, where they evolved into larger, faster, and more refined creatures that used their speed to escape predators. Their teeth evolved to allow them to graze efficiently. The number of toes gradually decreased.

By 10 to 25 million years ago, the animal evolved into Merychippus, which was the size of a Shetland pony and had fully adapted to open areas and grazing. Pliohippus, a

 Horses as Transportation

Dogs, trained to pull light carts, were the first animals that people used for work. About 4,000 years ago, cattle were used to pull wagons. They were bigger and stronger than dogs and could pull a lot more. Then someone discovered horses could do it even better. Horses were used for their meat and milk until perhaps 3,500 years ago, when it was discovered that they could pull more efficiently than the cow, and the animals' roles were reversed.

Nobody knows when someone first decided to sit on a horse, but as early as 3,000 years ago, horses were man's best form of transportation. The invention of horse shoes circa 900 A.D. helped make horses an even faster, more efficient means of transportation. Horses remained the world's primary means of transportation until less than 100 years ago.

This fossil of Mesohippus, a sheep-sized early ancestor of the horse, shows what the animal looked like during the Oligocene era.

faster horse about the size of a Welsh pony, was the next step up the evolutionary ladder. Appearing two to seven million years ago, it was very fast—much faster than its predecessors—in part because it had a solid single hoof on each foot.

Then, fewer than two million years ago, Equus first appeared. The first Equus resembled Przewalski's Horse, the last of the true wild horses. It was still hundreds of thousands of years before Equus began to resemble today's horses.

Over a period of 60 or 70 million years, the horse grew larger and faster. The back became straighter and the legs longer. The number of toes shrank to one, and its toenail formed the hoof. The teeth became suited for grazing.

The early ancestors of horses lived in the Western Hemisphere—what would later be called North and South

"Hot-blooded" horses like the Arab originated in a hot, dry climate where they did not need a heavy coat or excess fat. Bred for speed, these horses have thin skins and lightly muscled bodies that enable them to cool down quickly.

America. For reasons we will probably never know, they crossed the land bridge that once connected Asia and Alaska, leaving none in the Americas.

Early Equus was widespread throughout Europe, Asia, and North Africa. They migrated in herds in various directions and came upon varying conditions of climate and nutrition. These differences led to differences in appearance and disposition.

Most of these early widespread horses were of the same genus and species, Equus caballus. In some areas, however, other species of Equus evolved. In Africa, zebras, asses, and quaggas evolved. In Asia, Przewalski's Horse and the kiang and onager appeared. Each was uniquely suited to the specific environment.

The horses that inhabited the northern regions—Russia, Scandinavia, central Europe, and the British Isles—adapted to harsh winters. Their coats became thick and they carried a layer of fat. Grazing was good in these areas, and these horses became large, heavy, and strong, but not very fast. They didn't have to be fast to escape predators, because they had places to hide. The draft horses of today, such as the Percheron of France and the Shire of Great Britain, descend from these early heavy horses, and they are also known as cold-bloods. Draft horses are known for their strength and willingness to work, and they are often used for agricultural work.

Horses in the southern regions—Asia Minor and North Africa—evolved very differently. The climate was not cold, so these horses developed light, thin coats and carried no excess fat. Grazing was sparse, so they did not grow as large. With fewer places for concealment in the face of danger, speed was very important. They became very fast. These horses, referred to as hot-bloods, became riding and racing horses. Some common examples include the Arabian horse of Asia Minor and the Barb of North Africa.

These early breeds had no contact with other breeds, so they bred true. An Arabian bred to another Arabian produced an Arabian. There were no other breeds present in the area in which they developed. A Murakozi could only breed with another Murakozi in its native Hungary, so only more Murakozis were produced.

Then humans intervened, and, either accidentally or on purpose, the breeds from different parts of the world were brought together and interbred. Hot-bloods were bred to other hot-bloods, producing breeds like the Barb and Thoroughbred. Cold-bloods crossed with other cold-bloods produced new breeds, including the Clydesdale, the Shire, and the Percheron. Hot-bloods were also bred to cold-bloods, and vice-versa; the result of these crossings were called warm-bloods. Some examples are the Swiss Warmblood, the Swedish Warmblood, and the Dutch Warmblood.

Some early breeds and early crossings became popular and useful, but in time their popularity waned or their use was taken over by other or newer breeds or machines. Many of these breeds are now extinct or very rare.

But many of these new breeds proved to be better than their parents. Cross breds were bigger, stronger, faster, more agile or handy, or a more desirable color, or any of a myriad of other traits that man found to his liking. The best of these crossbreds were then bred to each other in the hope of producing a horse even better. Eventually these crosses bred true, that is, the desirable trait or traits appeared in subsequent generations. In this manner, new breeds were produced.

This is the way Secretariat's ancestors were created, as were the ancestors of all of today's pure breeds, or purebreds. Many people confuse the term "Thoroughbred" with the term "purebred." They are not interchangeable. A Thoroughbred is a purebred, but a purebred is not necessarily a Thoroughbred. Any horse whose ancestors are all of the same breed is called a purebred. A horse with different breeds in its recent background is called a cross bred, mixed-breed, or grade horse.

Purebred horses may be registered with a specific breed association or breed registry, which increases the horse's value, and its cost. However, mixed-breed horses are often just as suited to equestrian sports as purebred horses. While some horse sports, such as Quarter Horse or Thoroughbred racing, are restricted to a specific breed, other types of competition, including endurance riding, dressage, and eventing, are open to horses of all backgrounds and breeds.

2

Developed in England,
the Thoroughbred is now
found all over the world.
All modern Thoroughbreds
can trace their ancestry
to three founding sires:
the Darley Arabian, the
Godolphin Barb, and the
Byerly Turk.

HORSES OF THE BRITISH ISLES

M any of the breeds we are most familiar with today had their origins in the British Isles.

Thoroughbred

The Thoroughbred is one of the few breeds that has spread worldwide without crossing with local horses. Thoroughbreds make excellent riding, show jumping, and hunting horses, but the mention of the name "Thoroughbred" brings racing to everyone's minds.

Horseracing has always been popular. For centuries horse races have been staged all over the world using native breeds or crosses, but with the development of the Thoroughbred, breeding horses became both an art and a science. Three stallions brought to England in the late 17th and early 18th centuries are considered to be the foundation sires of the breed: the Darley Arabian, the Byerly Turk, and the Godolphin Barb.

The Darley Arabian was purchased at a Syrian horse market in 1704 by Thomas Darley, who gave the horse to his brother, who in turn stood him at stud, where he was bred to the best native mares in England. The greatest of all racehorses and sires, Eclipse, descended from him. Eclipse is the ancestor of thousands of great racehorses.

The Byerly Turk was brought to England in 1689 by Captain Byerly, who had captured one from the Turks at the Siege of Vienna. The great horse Herod descended from the Byerly Turk and many great horses trace to him in their pedigrees.

The Godolphin Barb was brought from Morocco around 1730 by Lord Godolphin. At first he was used only as a teaser, but eventually he was bred to a few mares and his offspring proved outstanding. One of his grandsons was Matchem, another great sire of racing Thoroughbreds, to which many of our present-day runners trace.

The Thoroughbred is a large horse, usually standing between 15.2 and 16.2 hands (one hand is equal to four inches) at the withers and weighing about 1,200 pounds. The head is small and the eyes are large. The neck is long and slightly arched, the back is long, the shoulder is sloped, the legs are long, the pasterns (the portions of the lower legs just above the hooves) are long and sloped, and the hooves are small.

Bay or brown is the main color, but chestnut, black, and gray are common. Roan, which is white hair mixed in with another color, and white are rare. White markings on the face and legs are usual, and occasionally there are small white markings on the body.

Welsh Pony

Welsh Ponies were developed in Wales. Their roots trace back more than 2,000 years. There are four recognized "types" of Welsh Pony, and the stud book is divided into four sections. Section A is the Welsh Mountain Pony, a small individual that may not be taller than 12.2 hands. Section B is the Welsh Pony, slightly larger than the Welsh Mountain Pony. They range in size from 12.2 to 13.2 hands. Section C is the Welsh Pony of Cob type, also not taller than 13.2 hands, but stockier and broader. Section D is the Welsh Cob, actually horse-sized, standing 14 to 15.1 hands.

The individuals of all four sections are used in the same manner. They are excellent riding ponies and there is a size for everyone. Welsh Ponies are ideal for children who have gotten too large for the smaller Welsh Mountain Pony. Sections A and B are good cart ponies, and all four types can handle light draft work.

The head is small, the eyes large and alert, the ears pricked, and the neck arched. The legs are sturdy and well muscled. Section C, the Welsh Pony of Cob type, is thicker-bodied and more muscular. All colors occur except piebald and skewbald.

Shetland Pony

The little Shetland Pony originated in the Shetland Islands of Scotland and is one of the oldest known breeds. Its ancestors may have come from Scandinavia around 8000 B.C. and they may have crossed with ponies later brought in by the Celts.

The Shetland is a popular riding pony for children, and it also excels at driving. Shetlands were once used in coal mines to haul carts.

The original use of Shetlands was as draft animals. They are much stronger than horses, pound for pound, and they were used extensively in coal mines. Eventually they became popular as a child's riding or harness pony. Their gentle disposition makes them ideal for these purposes.

The Shetland is the smallest of the pony breeds. The height may not exceed 42 inches (10.2 hands). All colors except spotted are acceptable.

Shire

The Shire is the largest breed, going back to the "great horse," the mount used in jousting and charging in medieval days. It is likely that an influx of Friesian blood occurred during the 16th century when that breed was brought in by Dutch engineers to work in draining the wetlands.

The Shire was important as a war horse because knights in armor weighed as much as 400 pounds and their mounts had to be very strong. In peace, the Shire was also important as a draft animal used to move goods from the docks inland.

A Shire is typically 17 to 18 hands, with some reaching 19 hands. A ton (2,000 pounds) is the normal weight, but larger ones may reach 3,000 pounds.

The head is small when compared with the body and the profile is slightly convex. The eyes and ears are large and the neck is long and well muscled. The legs are heavily muscled, and are feathered below the knees and hocks. The feet are huge and sound. Colors are bay, brown, black, gray, and chestnut, and white markings are common.

Once very common, the number of Shires has declined, but the breed is again gaining popularity among draft horse enthusiasts.

Connemara

This is a hardy pony that developed along the harsh western coast of Ireland. Ancient ponies inhabited this area and through the centuries Barbs, Arabians, and Andalusians were brought in and interbred with the native ponies, eventually producing the Connemara of today.

The Connemara ranges in size from 13 to 14.2 hands. They are excellent for riding as they are gentle and quite intelligent. They are also suited to harness or driving and are used for light draft work.

The head is attractive with a straight profile and small ears. The neck and back are long and the legs are sturdy and well muscled with long cannon bones. The original Connemaras were dun, but today gray, brown, bay, and black are also common. Colors such as chestnut and roan are rare.

Hackney and Hackney Pony

The Hackney breed arose in England shortly after the development of the Thoroughbred. Blaze, a Thoroughbred grandson of the Darley Arabian, sired a horse named Original Shales out of a Hackney mare around 1755. Original Shales was bred to Norfolk Trotter and Yorkshire Coach Horse mares and the resulting offspring became the modern Hackneys.

Norfolk Trotters and Yorkshire Coach Horses had been used as light work horses and carriage horses and, as such, were trotters, a gait at which the Hackney breed is most adept. The modern Hackney is used as a harness horse in horse shows. They are commonly called "Roadsters" or "Steppers" and are frequently the highlight of an evening's horse show classes.

Hackneys are black, brown, bay, or chestnut and may have white markings. The head and ears are small and the neck is long. The legs are medium in length with long, sloping pasterns. An average Hackney stands about 15 hands with a range of 14 to 16 hands.

The Hackney Pony is 12 to 14 hands and is the result of mating Hackneys to Fell and Welsh Ponies in the late 1800s. Their use is the same as Hackneys and they are included in the Hackney stud book. The introduction of pony blood has created a wider range of color. Hackney Ponies are black, brown, bay, gray, or roan, with or without white markings.

Clydesdale

The native draft horse of Lanarkshire, Scotland, was just not big enough or strong enough for the work being asked of it, so outside stallions were brought in to strengthen the breed. These were Belgian draft horses, Friesians, and a native stallion named Blaze (not the same one used in the development of Hackneys). Lanarkshire was formerly called Clydesdale, because the River Clyde flows through it, so that is how Clydesdales got their name. The breed was created there in the middle of the 16th century.

A Clydesdale mare and foal relax in their pasture. The Clydesdale is one of the largest draft breeds and is known for its feathered feet and high-stepping action.

Among the largest of all horses, the Clydesdale stands 16 to 18 hands and weighs more than a ton. Primarily used for farm work and heavy hauling, they were also used as carriage and war horses. Today they are best known as the "Budweiser horses."

They are gentle and willing with a strong, high head, wide between the eyes with a broad muzzle. The eyes, nostrils, and ears are large. The neck is long and arched. The legs and pasterns are long and strongly feathered, and the feet are large and tough. Bay is the preferred color with white legs.

Cleveland Bay

The Cleveland Bay is the oldest of the English horse breeds, dating back to at least 1700. First used as pack and light draft animals, they became excellent carriage horses, and hunters and jumpers, as well as riding mounts.

Cleveland Bays stand 16 to 16.2 hands and are bay with a black mane, tail, and legs. The only white allowed is a

 A Horse's Height

A horse's height is measured not at the top of the head as a person's is, but at the withers. The withers is the highest point of the back, where the neck meets the back. Height is not measured at a horse's head because getting a horse to hold its head as high as it can is difficult, but the withers is always in the same position. Height is measured in "hands," with each hand equalling four inches. The breeds range in height from more than 18 hands (over six feet at the withers) to less than 6 hands (shorter than two feet at the withers).

small star; gray hairs occur in the mane and tail of some strains. The head is medium sized and the profile is usually convex. The legs are medium with sloping pasterns.

Fell Pony

The Fell Pony developed from the breeding of Friesian stallions to local mares. The Friesians were brought to England around 55 B.C. by the Romans to use in the construction of Hadrian's Wall.

The Fell Pony stands 13 to 14 hands and is an excellent pack animal, but it is also quite good as a driving or riding horse. They are bay, brown, black, or gray. White markings are not desirable, although a small star and bits of white on the legs are accepted.

The head and ears are small and the back is long and straight. The legs are stocky and well muscled and the fetlocks are feathered. The mane and tail are heavy.

Dales Pony

Dales Ponies were originally used as pack horses and are very strong for their size. Native ponies, Friesians, and extinct Scottish Galloway Horses went into the makeup of the Dales Pony. From the Galloways the Dales Pony acquired its speed.

The breed almost died out during World War II, and by 1955 there were only four registered Dales Ponies. They have recovered and today are commonly used as riding and endurance horses.

The head and ears are small, the neck is short and muscular, the back is short, and the legs are short and feathered from the knees down. The mane and tail are thick. Colors are bay, brown, black, and gray, and white markings are uncommon. They stand 13.2 to 14.2 hands.

The Arab, or Arabian, is one of the oldest horse breeds in the world and has been interbred with many types of horses to improve bloodlines and create new breeds.

EASTERN HEMISPHERE BREEDS

Every country has developed horse breeds through the centuries. Some have become popular and lasting, while others fell into extinction after contributing to the creation or improvement of other breeds.

Arab

The Arab breed is one of the oldest (some say the oldest) pure breeds, although it did not originate in Arabia. The ancestors of the Arabian Horse came from the Middle Eastern countries of Jordan, Syria, Persia (known as Iran today), and other areas of northern Asia Minor.

Arabians are popular in all types of horse shows and sports, including western pleasure, saddle seat, and endurance riding.

Arabs have been used throughout the centuries in the development or improvement of almost every other breed. Arabs are by far the most widespread breed of all. Almost every country has an Arabian breed registry.

The Arabian horse is an intelligent, beautiful, medium-sized animal, standing 14 to 15 hands, and very willing to be trained and ridden. The main use of the breed is pleasure riding, but they are also used in the show ring, in endurance riding competitions, at which they excel, and as racehorses, although races for Arabs are quite long (three or four miles) and have not become very popular in the United States.

Coat color is gray, bay, chestnut, black, and occasionally roan, with white markings being common. The head is small and delicate, usually with a dished profile. The muzzle is small, the eyes are large, and the ears are small. The neck is long, the back is short, and the tail is carried high. The legs are muscular and the feet are small and tough.

Andalusian

The Andalusian has also been used widely to improve other breeds. As with most breeds, Andalusians have Arab blood through cross breeding in centuries past.

Andalusians are graceful, elegant, and fiery, yet calm and very tractable. The head has a slightly convex profile with small ears and alert, medium sized eyes. The neck is arched and the mane is long and wavy. The back slopes and the muscled legs have medium sized, strong hooves. They stand 15 to 16 hands.

Most Andalusians are gray, with chestnuts and a few bays occurring. They are excellent riding horses with high-stepping action.

Lipizzan

There are only about 3,000 Lipizzans in the world, with fewer than 500 in the United States, but it is one of the most famous breeds of all. These are the horses of the world-renowned Spanish Riding School of Vienna. During World War II the school and the Lipizzan horses were nearly destroyed. Fortunately, U.S. General George Patton put them under the care of the United States Army and they were saved.

A Lipizzaner from Lipica, Slovenia. Lipizzaners are dark colored when they are born, but get increasingly lighter with age. By age three they have begun to gray, and by the time they are ten they are pure white.

Austria protects the breed and is the only nation allowed to breed Lipizzans. The breeding is done at a large farm in Syria, and the colts are then sent to Austria.

Lipizzans are usually white or gray, but some browns do occur from time to time. They stand 15 to 16 hands tall. The head is long with a straight or slightly convex profile, the eyes are large, and the ears are small. The Lipizzan's neck is arched, its back is long, and its legs are extremely strong and muscled.

Trakhener

The Trakhener is a very versatile warm-blood breed. An excellent riding horse, it is also capable of endurance competition and light farm work. It is a large horse, usually standing at least 16 hands, and heavily muscled.

All colors occur in the breed, even piebald, although it is not desirable. The head is refined with a small muzzle; the neck is long and crested and the back is short.

Belgian

The Belgian is a huge draft horse, standing 16 to 17 hands and weighing a ton or more. The breed descended

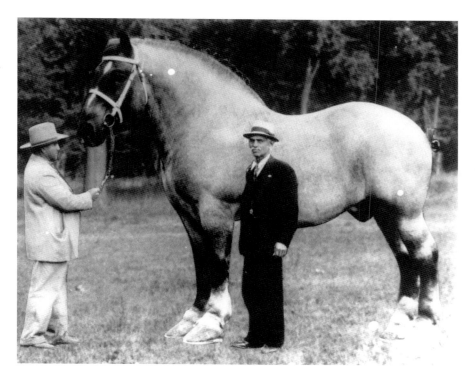

Born in 1928, the world's largest horse, Belgian stallion Brooklyn Supreme wore a 40" collar and had a girth of 10' 2". He weighed 3,200 pounds and stood 19$^{1}/_{2}$ hands.

from the Flemish "great horse" of medieval times, and was used to carry knights to the Crusades. Before farm machinery, these horses were extremely important to agricultural operations, and they continue to be used for farm work by the Amish. Belgians are also used in strength competitions and show hitches in the United States. In Europe, many are raised for meat.

Belgians are usually chestnut (also called sorrel), or red roan, but other colors are occasionally found. The head is light, the profile is straight or slightly concave, the eyes are large, and the ears are small. The neck and back are short and well muscled. The legs are thin compared to the body, but strong. There is some feathering at the fetlocks.

Percheron

The Percheron was developed in France centuries ago, and its development was greatly influenced by crosses with Arabs. The horse is a medium-sized draft animal, usually standing 15 to 16 hands and weighing 1,500 to 1,800 pounds. They are most often gray or black, and are used

Large and Small

The largest breed is the Shire, but the one largest horse of all time was a Belgian named Brooklyn Supreme. Foaled in 1928, he grew to 19^1/2 hands at the withers and weighed 3,200 pounds.

The smallest breed used to be the Shetland, but with the development of the Miniature Horse there became a new champion. There have been many Minis that stood 7 or more hands, but in 1895 one was foaled in England that grew to only 14^1/2 inches (a little over 3 hands).

today as show horses in strength exhibitions as well as work horses for agricultural purposes.

The head is fine, and the eyes are alert and active. The neck is long with a heavy mane and the back is short and straight. The legs are solid and powerful.

Norwegian Fjord Horse

Also called the Norwegian Fjord Pony, the modern breed has become larger than the ancient one. Long ago, they stood 12 hands, but today 13 to 14 hands is normal.

The Vikings used Norwegian Fjord Horses as mounts and rode them in war. They were also used for light farm work. They are always dun (a grayish yellow color) with a dark stripe on the back and zebra stripes on the legs. They have a wonderful disposition and are very trustworthy. Many are trained as jumpers, for which they are well suited.

The head is medium sized with a concave profile, the eyes are large, and the ears are small. The neck is short with a coarse mane that stands upright for a few inches. The back has a slight dip and the legs are short with a small amount of feathering at the fetlocks.

Icelandic Horse

This is one of the oldest pure breeds and although it is small—13 hands—it is officially a horse, not a pony. It is an intelligent, gentle horse, but very spirited and not a mount for children or inexperienced riders. It is a natural five-gaited horse. Slower maturing than most breeds, full growth is not reached until age seven. They shouldn't be ridden until at least age four.

The Icelandic Horse has a clean head with a straight profile. The neck is long. The legs are strong and muscled. All colors occur.

Hanoverian

The Hanoverian originated in Germany in the 17th century when Oriental, Spanish, and Neapolitan horses were crossed with local horses. The warm-blooded Hanoverian was originally developed as a cavalry mount.

Hanoverians are used extensively as show jumpers, but they are also riding and dressage horses. Many have been Olympic champions. They are large—16 to 17 hands. The head is plain with a straight profile. The neck is long. The overall impression a Hanoverian gives is strength. The most common colors are chestnut, bay, brown, black, and gray. White markings are usual.

Don

Today's Don breed was developed in the 18th and 19th centuries along the Don River in Russia. A very sturdy and strong large horse—15.2 to 17 hands—the Don was the mount of the Cossacks who drove Napoleon's army out of Russia in the early 1800s. The Don today is used primarily as a pleasure mount, but it is also capable of light draft work, jumping, and endurance riding.

The head is medium-sized with a slightly concave profile. The neck is medium length and the back is straight. Selective breeding in recent years has improved leg conformation, which was previously weak in the knees. The most common color is chestnut.

Gotland

This pony has existed on the island of Gotland off the Swedish coast since the Stone Age. Over the centuries there has been little change in the breed, which probably descended from the ancient forest horse of northern Europe. The Gotland is very similar to the Exmoor of

Holsteiners were originally heavy horses, but selective breeding with Thoroughbreds and Yorkshire Coach Horses helped lighten the breed, making it ideal for light harness and saddle work.

England and the two breeds likely developed in the same manner. The Exmoor is rare today.

Standing 11 to 13 hands, the Gotland is a hardy, durable, strong pony with great jumping ability and a natural trot. The head has a straight profile, large eyes, and small, erect ears. The neck is short, the back is long, and the legs are strong with long cannon bones (the bones from a horse's knees to its pasterns). Most are dun.

Holstein

The Holstein, or Holsteiner, is a warmblood breed from Germany and it dates back to at least the 13th century, when they were bred for cavalry mounts. In the 1700s and 1800s thousands were exported to other European countries.

The Holstein is a large, strong riding horse, sometimes standing more than 17 hands tall, and it excels as a show jumper. An intelligent, willing horse, it is sometimes used in the Olympic Games as a driving and dressage horse. Usual colors are bay, brown, and black. The head has a straight to slightly concave profile with bright eyes and alert ears. The neck is long and slightly arched and the back is long. The legs are short and stout.

Russian Heavy Draft Horse

The Russian Heavy Draft Horse developed in the Ukraine in the middle of the 19th century. It is a small draft horse, standing 14 to 15 hands, but is extremely strong and well muscled. The head is medium-sized with a straight profile. The neck is short and broad with a crest and the back is long. The legs are short and very muscular. Chestnut is the usual color, but bay and brown occur. They mature early and are willing workers.

Mongolian

The Mongolian may be the oldest pure breed in the world today. This hardy breed was used by Mongolian cavalry for centuries. Bred and raised in open fields year round with no supplemental feed, it is able to handle extremely cold weather. It is estimated that there are more than two million of the breed in Mongolia today.

A true all-purpose breed, it is used for riding, draft work, as a pack animal, and for its meat and milk. They come in all colors: bay, brown, black, gray, sorrel, dun, and even buckskin. Pony-sized (12 to 14 hands), the head is heavy, the neck short, and the body wide. The legs are short and stocky. The mane and tail are heavy and dense and there is excessive hair on the legs.

Akhal-Teke

This is a rare, medium-sized (14 to 16 hands), beautiful horse used for riding and racing. An ancient breed going back to at least the 8th century, it originated in Turkmenistan.

The Akhal-Teke is a thin horse with a straight, fine head. The neck is long and thin and the back is long. The legs are long and the feet are large. The most common color is shiny dun, but gray, black, and bay occur. White markings are common.

The Akhal-Teke's gait is almost a gliding movement, and the horse has great endurance. They are fairly slow to mature but live a long time. Though it was once near extinction, careful and selective breeding has brought the breed back. There are breeders in the United States now, and the Akhal-Teke is gaining popularity as a mount for endurance riding competitions.

Appaloosas take their name from "the Palouse," a region of the American Northwest that was once populated by Nez Perce Indians, who selectively bred the horses to be fast, strong, and sure footed.

BREEDS OF THE NEW WORLD

Horses first evolved in the Western Hemisphere, but they left millions of years ago, walking across the land bridge that once connected Asia to the Americas. Thus, the native inhabitants of the Americas did not have horses until Spanish explorers arrived in the "New World" in the 1500s, bringing horses with them. In this way, horses were reintroduced to their original homeland in the Americas.

The horse became essential to the development of the Americas. The people of the New World became true horse lovers and adapted the animals to their needs and desires. Many new breeds were created, especially in the United States.

The American Quarter Horse is known for being quick on its feet.
Quarter Horses have a fast, powerful take-off and a sprinting ability
that makes them ideal barrel racers.

American Quarter Horse

The American Quarter Horse is the United States' first
breed, both in origin and quantity. The American Quarter
Horse Association (AQHA) has approximately three million
horses registered and there are nearly a million AQHA members participating in shows and racing.

The Quarter Horse traces its roots to Spanish horses
brought to Florida in the 1500s. These were later crossed

with colonial horses brought from Europe, mainly England. The breed developed without input from Thoroughbreds, although much later Thoroughbred blood was used to refine the Quarter Horse.

The Quarter Horse takes its name from its ability as a racehorse. In the early colonies, there were no racetracks. Racing took place in the streets of towns and villages. These were, of course, short races. In time, the standard length came to be a quarter of a mile and the horses that ran in them were called "quarter horses." Because of their powerful hindquarters, Quarter Horses have a powerful take off and are among the fastest horses in the world for the first quarter of a mile. A Quarter Horse can even beat a Thoroughbred on a short track.

As westward expansion took place, Americans took their horses with them (or maybe it is better said that the horses took the Americans) and further talents were discovered for these Quarter Horses. They were excellent riding horses, they could serve as pack animals, and they were able to pull wagons.

Then someone came up with the idea of rounding up the herds of wild cattle that roamed the west. Here the Quarter Horse showed talent undoubtedly inherited from its Spanish ancestors that were used to work cattle in their native land. The Quarter Horses were quick and agile and could out-maneuver even the quickest cow.

Today they still work cattle, but they are used mainly for racing, pleasure, rodeo, and other horse shows. There are thousands of AQHA-sanctioned horse shows annually.

Approximately a third of all registered Quarter Horses are sorrel, but there are 13 recognized colors. Spotted markings, such as those of Pinto and Appaloosa Horses, are not allowed, but white markings are common.

"The American Quarter Horse," a painting by Orren Mixer, depicts the ideal American Quarter Horse.

Quarter Horses stand 14.2 to 16 hands, the larger size due to Thoroughbred influence. The head is small and short with bright, wide-set eyes, small, alert ears, and a straight profile. The neck is arched and muscular and the back is short and straight. The legs, especially the hind legs, are very muscular. The feet are small, actually appearing to be too small for a horse of this size.

American Saddlebred

Fanciers of the American Saddlebred call this high-stepping horse "the most beautiful breed in the world." The breed was developed in Kentucky (it was once called the Kentucky Saddler) by the pioneers, who wanted a quality horse, but one that had the stamina to take them over the mountains and valleys of colonial America while providing a comfortable ride. A wide variety of bloodlines went into the makeup of this horse, including Morgans, Narragansett Pacers, and Spanish horses. The American Saddlebred owes its many gaits to its varied ancestors.

The American Saddlebred is now used primarily as a five-gaited or three-gaited show horse or a fine harness horse. The five gaits are walk, trot, canter, rack, and slow gait, while in three-gaited horses it is only the first three.

The American Saddlebred stands 15 to 16 hands and is bay, chestnut, black, gray, and occasionally roan. White markings may occur. The head is finely chiseled with wide-set eyes and small ears set high on the head. The head is held high on a long, arched neck and the back is short. The tail is long and flowing. The pasterns are long and sloping and the feet are large.

Morgan

The Morgan is perhaps the only breed in history to descend from one single stallion. A 14-hand bay colt named Figure, foaled in 1789 in Massachusetts, was taken as payment of a debt by Justin Morgan, who took him to Vermont. Morgan tried to sell the colt, but found no takers because of his small size. Rented out to a neighbor, the little horse became a legend in a short time, out-performing all horses he was matched against at walking, trotting, running, or pulling. Legend says that Figure pulled more than horses weighing half again what he weighed.

Figure's ancestry is not known. Some claim he was sired by a Thoroughbred out of an Arab mare, but there is no proof. Upon the death of Justin Morgan, Figure came to be known by the name Justin Morgan.

As his fame spread, people wanted to breed their mares to him. These mares were of varied ancestry and type, but the resulting foals all bore a great resemblance to little Figure. Eventual breeding to larger mares to increase size did nothing to alter the appearance of the individuals. They all looked like Figure, only larger. Today Morgans stand between 14 and 15.2 hands.

The Morgan is a true multi-purpose breed, capable of being ridden, driven, jumped, or used for light draft work. It is a very alert, curious, and intelligent horse.

Bay and dark chestnut are the usual colors and white markings are not common. The expression is intelligent and the head is large though short. The eyes are prominent and the ears are short. The neck is muscular and the back is short and broad.

Tennessee Walking Horse

The Tennessee Walking Horse is seemingly made up of every breed of horse that passed through Tennessee. The breeds that went into creating this wonderful riding horse include Thoroughbred, Standardbred, Narragansett Pacer, Morgan, Canadian, American Saddlebred, and Spanish horses from Florida.

Developed by farmers in the late 1800s, the breed gained popularity as a riding horse. Today the Tennessee Walking Horse is used widely as a show horse, utilizing its three natural gaits: the flat-foot walk, the running walk, and the canter. These gaits make it a wonderful pleasure horse.

The horse stands 15 to 16 hands and comes in all colors, often with white markings. The head, once coarse, has become refined and is large with large eyes and ears. The neck is long and may be arched. The back is long and the tail sits high. The feet are large and substantial.

The Morgan horse is easily recognized by its upright neck and proud bearing.

Standardbred

These are the racing trotters and pacers. The breed traces its lineage to the Narragansett Pacer, the Morgan, and the Thoroughbred, which gave it size and refinement. The name Standardbred comes from a requirement of the breed's first stud book in 1871. To be registered, a horse had to trot or pace a mile in a standard time. Trotters had to do it in two minutes, 30 seconds, and pacers in two minutes, 25 seconds.

Although commonly thought of only as harness racers, Standardbreds are also pleasant riding horses. They stand

15 to 16 hands or slightly more. The head is somewhat coarse with a straight or slightly convex profile. The ears are long and the neck is short and straight. The back tends to be long. The mane and tail are long and thick.

Bay is the most common color, but brown, chestnut, black, and gray occur.

Appaloosa

The Appaloosa is considered an American breed, but ancient cave paintings in Europe and Asia clearly show horses with Appaloosa markings. The Indians of the West greatly liked these markings and selected for them in their horses. The Nez Perce of the Pacific Northwest were particularly attracted to these spotted horses. The area of the Palouse River was well known for these horses and a spotted horse became referred to as "a Palouse," which in time became Appaloosa.

At the time that the breed association was formed in 1938, both Arabs and Quarter Horses were allowed to be bred to Appaloosas, but now only registered Appaloosas may be used. The breed has become very popular, with more than half a million registered today. The one characteristic required of an Appaloosa is the "blanket," a white area of varying size on the rear (or the entire horse) that contains spots.

Used for pleasure riding and racing, they are generally 14.2 to 15.2 hands, but some reach 16 hands.

The head is small with a straight profile and large eyes surrounded by white sclera, or outer eye membranes. The ears are pointed and the neck is long and slightly arched. The back is straight and the legs are large boned. The hooves are black and white striped. The skin of the nose, lips, and genitals is mottled.

Despite their small size, miniature horses are popular driving horses with the strength to pull an adult in a wheeled carriage.

American Miniature

This is the only breed with a size limitation: they may be no taller than 34 inches (8.2 hands). In confirmation and proportion, Miniatures look like horses, only smaller. They are not ponies.

They probably descended from English and Dutch mine ponies that were imported to work in Appalachian coal mines, with the Shetland contributing to the development of the breed.

All known horse colors and patterns occur in the breed. Their use is as pets and as small cart horses. Too small to ride, they are intelligent, curious, and kind, and they have been used in therapeutic programs for the disabled and the aged.

Paso Fino

Named for its movement, Paso Fino means "fine gait" in Spanish. The breed originated in Puerto Rico and other Latin American countries and possibly resulted from crosses of the extinct Spanish Jennet with Andalusians. Paso Finos first entered the United States around 1950.

The Paso Fino stands 14 to 15 hands and is very docile. The head is small with a slightly convex profile and large, wide-set eyes. The neck is medium length, upright, and slightly arched. The legs are delicate and the hooves are small. The mane and tail are allowed to grow long and full.

The gait for which it is named is very smooth and comfortable for the rider. The horse is used primarily for pleasure riding, but is also shown.

Pony of the Americas

This is a new breed that had its beginnings in 1954 with a foal by a Shetland stallion out of an Appaloosa mare. Later there were crosses to Arabs, Quarter Horses, Welsh Ponies, and Shetlands. The result is a pony standing 11.2 to 13 hands with Appaloosa markings.

Possessing a quiet disposition, a Pony of the Americas (POA) is strong, fast, and durable. It is an excellent riding pony for both children and adults and is also used for dressage, jumping, and showing.

The head has a slightly concave profile, large eyes with white sclera, and medium sized, pricked ears. The neck is slightly arched, the back is short, and the legs are solid and well muscled. The hooves are striped like the Appaloosa's.

Palomino

Palomino is a color, not a breed, and the whole world has known Palominos for centuries, but it was in the United

The American Paint Horse comes in two color patterns: overo and tobiano. the stallion on the left has a coat in a chestnut overo pattern, while the gelding on the right is a bay roan tobiano.

States that breed registries for this horse were formed. The Palomino color—golden with a white mane and tail and dark or hazel eyes—occurs in most breeds, with the most notable exception being the Thoroughbred. For this reason, there are no standard physical characteristics associated with these horses. They come in all sizes and shapes.

Breeding for the Palomino color is difficult. The best chance for getting a Palomino foal is to breed a Palomino to a chestnut. A Palomino bred to any other color usually produces different coloring from either parent, but not another Palomino.

American Paint

Unlike the Palomino, which is only a color, the American Paint Horse is a breed with color requirements.

Paint Horses are far from American in origin. Like the Appaloosa, they are depicted in cave paintings. They were common in ancient China. The Egyptians left behind many paintings of them. They were a favorite mount of the Huns, and they were popular in Spain. Once introduced to this continent, they gained popularity with Indians because their coloring was beneficial in camouflage.

Today, the American Paint is a very versatile animal, being used in stock work, as a riding horse, as a show horse, and for racing.

There are two color patterns: overo and tobiano. They are differentiated by the location of white on the horse. The overo has white across the back, a white face, and dark legs. The tobiano's head is marked as a solid colored horse's, although there may be a star or a stripe, and all four legs are usually white.

Outcrosses are permitted to Quarter Horses and Thoroughbreds, and the American Paint is of a similar size—15 to 16 hands. The head is attractive with a straight profile, large eyes, and average sized ears. The neck and legs are muscular, and the back is short.

 Love Those Spots

There is something about spotted horses and ponies that humans have always liked. Pictures of horses with spotted markings appear on the walls of ancient caves, and horses and ponies with unusual markings were highly prized by Native Americans. In the early 20th century, itinerant photographers traveled the eastern United States with spotted ponies and cameras. In the days before instant and disposable cameras, parents hired photographers to take a photo of their child sitting on a pony. The contrasting colors of spotted ponies showed up especially well in black and white photography.

Peruvian Paso

"Paso" means "gait" in Spanish and this horse has a wonderfully smooth gait that makes it a superior riding horse. It is a natural gait that does not have to be taught. The breed is becoming increasingly popular in the United States.

Originating from Spanish horses crossed with later imports of other breeds, the Peruvian Paso at one time had a wide diversity in type, but careful breeding has developed it into what it is today.

A small horse, standing 14 to 15 hands, it comes in all colors with or without white markings. The head is small and thin with a straight or slightly convex profile. The eyes are wideset and round and the ears are short. The neck is short, thick, and arched, and the back is of medium length and slightly dipped. The legs have a short forearm and long cannons in front, with short cannons in the hindlegs.

Rocky Mountain Horse

This breed originated in Kentucky in the early 1900s but a registry wasn't formed until the mid-1980s. The foundation sire of the Rocky Mountain Horse was a stallion of undetermined ancestry named Old Tobe, who was gentle enough for kids to ride. This gentleness is a prime quality of the breed. Old Tobe also possessed the gait that makes these horses so comfortable to ride. In recent years the breed has gained popularity and ias a trail and endurance horse. Most Rocky Mountain Horses are 12 to 15 hands, but some reach 16 hands. The color of choice is dark chestnut, with a flaxen mane and tail, but any solid color is okay. White on the legs may not go above the knees or hocks.

The head is medium sized with bright, alert eyes and medium sized ears. The neck is medium and slightly arched and the back is short. The hooves are sound.

Zebras are black and white striped members of the horse family native to eastern and southern Africa. While running with the herd, the zebra's stripes function as camouflage; predators are confused by the tangle of stripes and are often unable to focus on an individual prey.

MEMBERS OF THE HORSE FAMILY

U ntil now, all the animals covered in this book have belonged to the same species, Equus caballus. Other members of the genus are different species.

Przewalski's Horse

Until recently it was believed that this wild horse of Asia was discovered in the 1880s, but it was found recently to have been described in unpublished manuscripts written in the 1400s. (By "discovered," we mean known to the Western World. The people who have lived in the areas inhabited by the Przewalski's Horse knew it was there all along.)

The name is pronounced "sha-VAL-ski." Attempts to tame them were unsuccessful for years, but lately photographs have appeared of a few Przewalski's Horses being ridden. Still, it is not an animal destined to be a backyard pet. Historically they have been hunted for meat and not used in any other way.

There have been several experiments in breeding Przewalski's Horses to domestic horses, mostly in Russia, to see if a useful animal such as the mule could be created. The resulting offspring have not proven satisfactory.

In color, size, and shape, the Norwegian Fjord closely resembles the primitive Przewalski's Horse.

The Przewalski's Horse stands 12 to 14 hands and has a large, heavy head with a straight profile, small eyes, and large ears. The neck is short and broad and has a short, upright mane. The back is long and straight and the legs are short with short pasterns. The hoof is long and narrow. The tail is tufted at its end.

All of the species are yellowish dun with a dark mane and tail and a dark stripe on the back. The lower legs have zebra stripes. White markings do not occur.

Tarpan

Also known as the European wild horse, the last wild Tarpan was accidentally killed in 1879 while attempts were being made to capture it. The last one in captivity died in a German zoo in 1887.

An extremely ancient breed that once roamed western Russia, it had been hunted into extinction as a source of meat. Light horses that developed in those regions probably descended from it.

The Tarpan that exists today is the result of attempts to reconstruct the animal by using its nearest existing relatives, most notably the Polish Konik, believed to be a direct descendent of the original Tarpan. These "new" Tarpans look like the old ones, but they are not the same.

They stand about 13 hands and are used for riding and light draft. They are always some shade of dun with a dark stripe on the back and zebra stripes on the upper legs. The mane, tail, and lower legs are black.

The head is long and broad with a straight or convex profile. The eyes are small and round and the ears are long and point somewhat to the side. The neck is short and thick with a full mane and the back is long and straight. The legs are long and slender.

Horses belong to an ancient family of animals known as ungulates, the first mammals to develop hooves. They are related to another ungulate, the rhinoceros. All ungulates are plant eaters with keen senses of hearing and smell.

Zebra

There are three different species of zebra and all are native to Africa, but they are all striped differently.

The mountain zebra (Equus zebra) is silver-white and has black stripes on all of its body except the stomach and the inner part of the thighs. The markings on the head are brown and the muzzle is tannish-bay. They stand about 12 hands. The large head has a straight to slightly convex profile, and the ears are long. The neck is short and has a short, erect mane. The legs are short and thin. The tail is tufted at the end. This species is endangered due to hunting.

The plains zebra (Equus quagga) is still plentiful, but it too is hunted. It looks much like the mountain zebra although slightly taller, but instead of white it is cream to light yellow with broad black stripes interspersed with fainter markings called shadow stripes. There are several variations in the stripe pattern, and some of these are classified as subspecies. Some refer to them as quaggas, but the true quagga (Equus quagga) was driven to extinction in the 19th century. The quagga was of a darker color and had stripes only on its head, neck, and shoulders. It was more of a forest dweller.

The third species, Grevy's zebra (Equus grevyi), is named for a former president of France, Jules Grevy. It is the largest of the three species, standing up to 15 hands. It is white with numerous narrow stripes, but otherwise resembles the mountain zebra. Unfortunately, it is almost extinct.

Zebras were long thought to be untamable, but now there are recorded cases of a few being broken to ride. Generally, however, they are not agreeable to handling of any sort.

 ## Mules

A hybrid is a cross between two species. Mules are hybrids of a jackass and a mare. The head, ears, and tail look like an ass, but the size is that of a horse. Mules are very strong, surefooted, long-lived, and stubborn. They are excellent work and riding animals.

Once thought to be sterile, some female mules and a few males have been found to be fertile.

A stallion bred to a jenny produces a hinny. It has a bushier tail and a heavier body than a mule and is more willing, but not as strong.

Ass

The ass is also known as the donkey, and, in the United States, the burro, although the burro is usually a miniaturized version.

The African wild ass (Equus asinus) was probably domesticated around 4000 B.C. by the Egyptians. They were used for riding, as pack animals, to pull carts and wagons, and for light draft work, just as they are today. They are more easily tamed and taught than most horses and are much more surefooted, making them superior on mountain paths.

They have medium-sized heads with a straight to slightly convex profile, small eyes, and very long ears. They are always gray with whitish under parts and muzzle and a black stripe on the back. There is a short, erect mane and a tuft of long hair on the end of the tail. They usually stand about 12 hands, although those called burros are often smaller. They are fast (up to 30 mph) and live long (30 to 50 years).

The Asian wild ass (Equus hemionus) lives in the desert areas of Mongolia, is taller than the African wild ass (about 13 hands), and has much shorter ears. The color is usually reddish-brown, but may be gray or yellowish, otherwise it looks quite like its African cousin. It can reach speeds of 45 mph and can maintain a pace of 15 mph for up to two hours.

There are two other species of wild asses in Asia, the kiang (Equus kiang), which lives on the high plateaus of Tibet, and the onager (Equus onager), also known as the Persian wild ass, which lives in northern Asia Minor.

All species of ass are hunted for meat and their hides, which make good leather. There are believed to be only about 3,000 African wild asses left, but in Mongolia the Asian wild ass may number that many in one herd.

The donkey, or ass, comes in all shapes and sizes and is used as a draft and pack animal, a stable companion, and as a sure-footed mount.

Unlike the horse, which carries its young 11 months or slightly longer, asses have a pregnancy length of a year to 13 months. The male is called a jack, or jackass, and the female is called a jenny.

The horse breeds and the different species in the horse family that we have discussed in these five chapters are by no means all there are. They are merely the most common or most popular, and from these the reader can get an idea of the tremendous variety among horses and the many different uses of the horse breeds.

Table of World Horse Breeds

Breed	Origin	Breed	Origin	Breed	Origin
EQUUS CABALLUS		Bavarian Warmblood	Germany	Cirit	Turkey
Abtenauer	Austria	Belgian Ardennais	Belgium	Cleveland Bay	England
Abyssinian	Ethiopia	Belgian Country Bred	Belgium	Clydesdale	Scotland
Adaev	Kazakhstan	Belgian Draft	Belgium	Colombian Criollo	Colombia
Akhal-Teke	Turkmenistan	Belgian Halfblood	Belgium	Colorado Ranger	USA
Albanian	Albania	Belgian Warmblood	Belgium	Comtois	France
Albino	USA	Bhirum	Nigeria	Connemara	Ireland
Algerian Barb	Algeria	Bhutia	India	Corsican	France
Altai	Siberia	Black Sea Horse	Russia	Costa Rican	
Alter Real	Portugal	Bobo	Ivory Coast	Saddle Horse	Costa Rica
American Bashkir Curly	USA	Bornu	Nigeria	Costeno	Peru
American Indian Horse	USA	Bosnia	Yugoslavia	Cuban Paso	Cuba
American Miniature	USA	Boulonnais	France	Cuban Pinto	Cuba
American Mustang	USA	Brandenburg	Germany	Cuban Trotter	Cuba
American Paint Horse	USA	Brazilian Sport Horse	Brazil	Cukorova	Turkey
American Quarter Horse	USA	Breton	France	Czech Coldblood	Czechoslovakia
American Saddlebred	USA	British Appaloosa	England	Czechoslovakian	
American Shetland	USA	British Riding Pony	England	Small Riding Horse	Czechoslovakia
American Walking Pony	USA	British Spotted Pony	England	Czechoslovakian	
Andalou	Turkey	British Warmblood	England	Trotter	Czechoslovakia
Andalusian	Spain	Brumby	Australia	Czech Warmblood	Czechoslovakia
Andean	Peru	Buckskin	USA	Dabrowa-Tarnowska	Poland
Anglo-Kabarda	Caucasus	Budyonny	Russia	Dagestan	Russia
Anglo-Karachai	Russia	Bulgarian Heavy Draft	Bulgaria	Dahoman	Poland
Annamese	Vietnam	Bulgarian Mountain Pony	Bulgaria	Dales Pony	England
Appaloosa	USA	Buohai	China	Danish Oldenborg	Denmark
AraApaloosa	USA	Buryat	Buryotia	Danisj Sport Pony	Denmark
Arab	Middle East	Byelorussian Harness	Byelorussia	Danish Warmblood	Denmark
Araba	Turkey	Calabrian	Italy	Danubian	Bulgaria
Argentine Criollo	Argentina	Camargue	France	Dartmoor Pony	England
Argentine Polo Pony	Argentina	Cambodian	Cambodia	Datong	China
Assateague/Chincoteague	USA	Campeiro	Brazil	Deccani	India
Asturian	Spain	Campolina	Brazil	Deli-Orman	Bulgaria
Australian Pony	Australia	Canadian	Canada	Deliboz	Azerbaijan
Australian Stock Horse	Australia	Canadian Cutting Horse	Canada	Djerma	Niger
Austrian Warmblood	Austria	Canadian Pinto	Canada	Dobrogea	Romania
Auxois	France	Canadian Rustic Pony	Canada	Dole Gudbrandsdal	Norway
Avar	Russia	Canadian Sport Horse	Canada	Dolny-Iskar	Bulgaria
Avelignese	Italy	Canik	Turkey	Don	Russia
Azerbaijan	Azerbaijan	Cape Horse	South Africa	Dongola	Cameroon
Azores	Azores, Portugal	Capitanata	Italy	Dulmen Pony	Germany
Azteca	Mexico	Carpathian Pony	Poland, Romania	Dutch Draft	Holland
Bagual (feral horse)	Argentina	Carthusian	Spain	Dutch Tuigpaard	Holland
Bahr-el-Ghazal	Chad	Caspian	Iran	Dutch Warmblood	Holland
Baise	China	Cerbat	USA	East and Southeast Anadolu	Turkey
Balearic	Spain	Chakouyi	China	East Bulgarian	Bulgaria
Bali	Indonesia	Chara Horse	Russia	East Friesian	Germany
Balikun	China	Cheju	Korea	East Friesian Warmblood	Germany
Baluchi	Pakistan	Chikasaw	USA	Elegant Warmblood	Germany
Banamba	Mali	Chilean	Chile	Eleia	Greece
Banar	Romania	Chilote	Chile	English Cob	England
Bandiagara	Niger	Chinese Kazakh	China	English Hack	England
Ban-ei Race Horse	Japan	Chinese Mongolian	China, Mongolia	English Hunter	England
Banker Horse	USA	Chola	Peru	English Thoroughbred	England
Bardigiano	Italy	Chumbivilcas	Peru	Eriskay Pony	Scotland
Bashkir	Russia	Chummarti	Tibet	Erlunchun	China
Basuto	Lesotho	Chumysh	Russia	Esperia Pony	Italy
Batak	Indonesia	Chyanta	Nepal	Estonian Draft	Estonia

Table of World Horse Breeds

Breed	Origin	Breed	Origin	Breed	Origin
Estonian Native	Estonia	Irish Hunter	Ireland	Manipuri	India
Exmoor	England	Israeli	Israeli	Maremmana	Italy
Faeroe Island Horse	Denmark	Java	Indonesia	Marwari	India
Falabella	Argentina	Jianchang	China	Mazari	Afghanistan
Fell Pony	England	Jielin	China	Mazuri	Poland
Finnhorse	Finland	Jimhong	China	Mbai	Chad
Fleuve	Senegal	Jinzhou	China	Megezh	Yakutia
Flores	Indonesia	Jutland	Denmark	Megrel	Georgia
Florida Cracker Horse	USA	Kabarda	Caucasus	Merens	France
Fouta	Senegal	Kabuli	India	Messara	Greece
Frederiksborg	Denmark	Kalmyk	Astrakhan, Volgograd	Mezen	Russia
Freiberg	Switzerland	Karabair	Uzbekistan	Mezohegyes Sport Horse	Hungary
French Anglo-Arab	France	Karabakh	Azerbaijan	Mijertinian	Somalia
French Ardennais	France	Karacabey	Turkey	Minusin	Russia
French Cob	France	Karachai	Caucasus	Mira Pony	Portugal
French Saddle Pony	France	Karakacan	Turkey	Misaki	Japan
French Trotter	France	Karakachan	Bulgaria	Missouri Fox Trotter	USA
Friesian	Holland	Kathiswari	India	Miyako	Japan
Furioso	Hungary	Kazakh	Kazakhstan	Moldavian	Romania
Galiceno	Mexico	Ke-Er-Qin	China	Mongolian	Mongolia
Garrano	Portugal	Khakassk	Russia	Morab	USA
Gelderland	Holland	Kielce	Poland	Morgan	USA
German Riding Pony	Germany	Kiger Mustang	USA	Moroccan Barb	North Africa
Giawf	Yemen	Kirdi Pony	Chad	Mossi	Ivory Coast
Gidran	Hungary	Kirgiz	Kirgizia	Moyle Horse	USA
Gotland	Sweden	Kisber Halfbred	Hungary	Murakoz	Hungary, Yugoslavia
Griffin	Mongolia	Kiso	Japan	Murghese	Italy
Groningen	Holland	Kladruby	Czechoslovakia	Mustang	USA
Guanzhong	China	Knabstrup	Denmark	Mytilene	Turkey
Guizhou	China	Konik	Poland	Nagdi	Yemen
Guoxia	China	Koto-Koli Pony	Benin	Namib desert Horse	Namibia
Hackney	England	Kushum	Kazakhstan	Narym	Siberia
Hackney Pony	England	Kustanai	Kazakhstan	National Appaloosa Pony	USA
Haflinger	Austria	Kuznet	Siberia	National Show Horse	USA
Hailar	China	Landais	France	National Spotted Saddle Horse	USA
Half Saddlebred	USA	Latvian	Latvia	Native Mexican	Mexico
Hanoverian	Germany	Lewitzer	Germany	Nefza	Tunisia
Hausa	Niger	Lezgian	Russia	New Forest Pony	England
Heihe	China	Libyan Barb	Libya	Newfoundland Pony	Canada
Heilongkiang	China	Lichuan	China	New Kirgiz	Kirgizia
Hequ	China	Lijiang	China	Nigerian	Nigeria
Herati	Afghanistan	Lipizzan	Austria	Nogal	Somalia
Hessen	Germany	Liptako	Ivory Coast	Noma	Japan
Highland	Scotland	Lithuanian Heavy Draft	Lithuania	Nonius	Hungary
Hinis	Turkey	Ljutomer Trotter	Yugoslavia	Nooitgedacht	South Africa
Hispano-Bretona	Spain	Llanrero	Venezuela	Noriker	Austria
Hirzal	Pakistan	Lokai	Tadzhikistan	Northeastern	Brazil
Hodh	Mali	Lundy Pony	England	Northern Ardennais	France
Hokkaido	Japan	Lusitano	Portugal	Northlands Pony	Norway
Holstein	Germany	M'Bayar	Senegal	North Swedish Horse	Sweden
Hungarian Coldblood	Hungary	M'Par	Senegal	North Swedish Trotter	Sweden
Hungarian Dun	Hungary	Macedonian	Yugoslavia	Norwegian Fjord	Norway
Hungarian Sport Horse	Hungary	Madagascan Pony	Madagascar	Oldenburg	
Icelandic Horse	Iceland	Makra	Pakistan	(Modern and Old types)	Germany
International Striped Horse	USA	Malakan	Turkey	Oriental Horse	Middle East
Iomud	Turkmenistan	Malopolski	Poland	Orlov Trotter	Russia
Irish cob	Ireland	Mangalarda Marchador	Brazil	Palomino	USA
Irish Draft	Ireland	Mangalarda Paulista	Brazil	Panje	Poland, Russia

Table of World Horse Breeds

Breed	Origin	Breed	Origin	Breed	Origin
Pantaneiro	Brazil	Shire	England	Turkoman	Turkmenistan
Paso Fino	Puerto Rico	Silesian	Poland	Tushin	Georgia
Patibarcina	Cuba	Sini	China	Tuva	Siberia
Pechora	Russia	Skyros	Greece	Ukrainian Saddle Horse	Ukraine
Peneia	Greece	Slovak Mountain	Czechoslovakia	Unmol	India
Percheron	France	Slovak Warmblood	Czechoslovakia	Uzunyayla	Turkey
Periangan	Indonesia	Sokolka	Poland	Vladimir Heavy Draft	Vladimir
Persia Arab	Iran	Somali Pony	Somalia	Voronezh Coach Horse	Russia
Peruvian Paso	Peru	Songhai	Mali, Niger	Vyatka	Kirov, Udmurtia
Petiso Argentino	Argentina	Sorraia	Portugal, Spain	Waler	Australia
Petite Boulonnais	France	South African Miniature	South Africa	Waziri	Pakistan
Philippine Pony	Philippines	South German Coldblood	Germany	Wielkopolski	Poland
Pindos	Greece	Southwest Spanish Mustang	USA	Welera	USA
Pinto	USA	Soviet Heavy Draft	Russia	Welsh: Cob, Mountain Pony,	
Piquira Pony	Brazil	Spanish-American Horse	Spain,	Pony, Pony of Cob Type	Wales
Pleven	Bulgaria	Americas		Western Sudan Pony	Sudan
Poitou Mule Producer	France	Spanish Anglo-Arab	Spain	Westphalian	Germany
Polesian	Byelorussia, Ukraine	Spanish Barb	USA	Wurttemberg	
Polish Draft	Poland	Spanish Colonial Horse	USA	(Modern and Old types)	Germany
Poljakoff	Mongolia	Spanish Mustang	USA	Xilingol	China
Pony Mousseye	Cameroon	Spanish Trotter	Majorca, Spain	Yabu	Afghanistan
Pony of the Americas	USA	Spiti	India	Yagha	Ivory Coast
Pottok	Spain, France	Standardbred	USA	Yakut	Siberia
Priob	Siberia	Stara Planina	Bulgaria	Yanqi	China
Puno Pony	Chile	Stuhm	Poland	Yemen Horse	Yemen
Rahvan	Turkey	Suffolk	England	Yemeni Horse	Yemen, Arabia
Rajshahi	Bangladesh	Sulawesi	Indonesia	Yili	China
Rhineland Heavy Draft	Germany	Sulebawa	Nigeria	Yiwu	China
Rila Mountain	Bulgaria	Sumba	Indonesia	Yugoslav Draft	Yugoslavia
Rocky Mountain Horse	USA	Sunbawa	Indonesia	Yugoslav Mountain Pony	Yugoslavia
Rodopi	Bulgaria	Swedish Ardennes	Sweden	Yonaguni	Japan
Romanian Saddle Horse	Romania	Swedish Warmblood	Sweden	Yunnan	China
Romanian Traction Horse	Romania	Swiss Warmblood	Switzerland	Zaniskari	India
Rottal	Germany	Syrian Arab	Syria	Zhemaichu	Lithuania
Royal Canadian		Sztum	Poland	Zobnatica Halfbred	Yugoslavia
Mounted Police Horse	Canada	Taishsuh	Japan		
Russian Heavy Draft	Ukraine	Tajik	Russia	***OTHER SPECIES***	
Russian Saddle Horse	Russia	Tanghan	Nepal	Ass	
Russian Trotter	Russia	Tarai	Nepal	African Wild Ass	
Sable Island Horse	Canada	Tattu	Nepal	(E. asinus)	North Africa
Sacz	Poland	Tavda	Russia	Asian Wild Ass	
Sahel	Mali	Tennessee Walking Horse	USA	(E. hemionus)	Mongolia
Salerno	Italy	Tersk	Russia	Kiang (E. kiang)	Tibet
Sandalwood	Indonesia	Thai Pony	Thailand	Onager (E. onager)	Iran
Sandan	China	Thessalian	Greece	Przewalski's Horse	
Sanfratello	Italy	Tibetan	Tibet, China	(E. przewalski poliakov)	Mongolia
Sanhe	China	Tieling	China	Tarpan	
Sardinian Anglo-Arab	Italy	Timor	Indonesia	(E. przewalski gmelini)	Poland, Russia
Sardinian Pony	Italy	Tokara	Japan	Zebra	
Sarvar	Hungary, Austria	Tolfetana	Italy	Grevy's (E. grevyi)	Eastern Africa
Schleswig	Germany	Tori	Estonia	Mountain (E. zebra)	South Africa
Schwarzwalder Fuchse	Germany	Torodi	Niger	Plains (E. quagga)	Central Africa
Selle Francais	France	Trakehner	Germany		
Senne	Germany	Trakya	Turkey		
Shagya Arabian	Hungary	Transylvanian	Romania		
Shami	Yemen	Transylvanian Lowland	Romania		
Shan	Burma	Trote en Gallope	Colombia		
Shetland	Scotland	Tunisian Barb	Tunisia		

GLOSSARY

Bay—a horse color, ranging from light brown to deep reddish-brown with black mane, tail, and lower legs

Browser—a vegetarian animal that moves about as it feeds

Buckskin—a horse color, ranging from light to dark tan with black mane, tail, and lower legs

Cannons or cannon bones—the bones in a horse's legs from the knees, or hocks, to the pasterns

Chestnut—a horse color, reddish-brown with mane, tail, and lower legs of the same color

Dun—a horse color, any of the various shades of tan with a black mane, tail, and lower legs, and a black or dark stripe down the back; the legs often have zebra stripes

Feathers or feathering—long hair on the legs or pasterns of some breeds of horse

Fetlock—the joint where the cannon bone joins the pastern in a horse's lower leg

Hand—unit of measure used to determine the height of a horse, equal to four inches

Hybrid—the offspring of two different species

Pastern—the portion of a horse's lower leg between the foot and the fetlock joint

Piebald—a horse color, white and black spots

Purebred—a breed of animal that has ancestors of the same breed

Roan—a horse color, yellowish- or reddish-brown sprinkled with gray

Sclera—the white outer membrane of the eye, except that which is covered by the cornea

Skewbald—a horse color, white and brown spots

Stud book—the term for the registry of purebred animals

Teaser—a stallion used for the purpose of determining when mares are ready to breed, but not himself used as a breeding animal

Ames, Fran A. *The Big Book of Horses: The Illustrated Guide to More Than 100 of the World's Best Breeds.* Philadelphia: Courage Books, 1999.

Draper, Judith. *The Book of Horses: An Encyclopedia of Horse Breeds of the World.* New York: Lorenz Books, 2000.

Edwards, Elwyn Hartley. *Ultimate Horse Book.* Columbus, Missouri: DK Publishing, 1991.

Hendricks, Bonnie L. *International Encyclopedia of Horse Breeds.* Norman, Oklahoma: University of Oklahoma Press, 1995.

Kidd, Jane, editor. *The International Encyclopedia of Horses and Ponies.* New York: Howell Book House, 1995.

BRENT KELLEY is an equine veterinarian and writer. He is the author of many books on baseball history. Two books (written under the pen name Grant Kendall) tell about his experiences as a veterinarian. He has also written four books for Chelsea House Publishers. He is a columnist for *Thoroughbred Times*, a weekly horse racing and breeding publication. He also writes for *Bourbon Times*, a weekly family newspaper. Brent Kelley has written more than 400 articles for magazines and newspapers. He lives in Paris, Kentucky, with his wife, children, and horses.